BY THE SAME AUTHOR

Looking Toward Inis Oírr (South Tipperary Arts 2004)
Amour Improper (Hub Editions 2005)
Sea of Leaves (Waterloo Press 2009)

Night Walk

JOHN McKEOWN

salmonpoetry

Published in 2011 by
Salmon Poetry
Cliffs of Moher, County Clare, Ireland
Website: www.salmonpoetry.com
Email: info@salmonpoetry.com

Copyright © John McKeown, 2011

ISBN 978-1-907056-68-0

All rights reserved. No part of this publication may be reproduced or transmitted in any form or by any means, electronic or mechanical, including photography, recording, or any information storage or retrieval system, without permission in writing from the publisher. The book is sold subject to the condition that it shall not, by way of trade or otherwise, be lent, resold or otherwise circulated without the publisher's prior consent in any form of binding or cover other than that in which it is published and without a similar condition, including this condition, being imposed on the subsequent purchaser.

COVER IMAGE: Underwater Night © Rolffimages | Dreamstime.com
COVER DESIGN: Siobhán Hutson

Salmon Poetry receives financial support from The Arts Council

"I understand the night, why should I seek the light?"

ALEISTER CROWLEY

Acknowledgements

Thanks are due to the editors of the following journals in which some of these poems have previously appeared: *Southword Online, The Shop, Borderlines, The Moth, The Recusant* website, *Equinox, The Frogmore Papers, Other Poetry*, and *Grasp*.

Contents

Winter	11
Twilight	12
Cadence	13
Nocturne	14
The Passing Sky	15
Cornwall Winter	16
Winter	17
Searching	18
Flowing Away	19
Odalisque	20
The Wild Sea	21
Unfolding	22
Hedgehog	23
Spring Rain	24
Candleflame	25
Black Bird	26
Wood-Pigeon	27
Clipped	28
Gods	29
Moth	30
Unconscientious Objector	31
Duality	32
Emptiness	33
No More Black Magic	34
The Fog Horn	35
Honeycomb	36
Backbone of the Nation	37
Conversation	38
Sunset	39
Orienteering	40
Salute to Li Po	41
Loophole	42

Underworld	43
Arboreal Meditation	44
Florescence	45
Aphrodite Dictates	46
The Unbleached Blonde	47
Rosary	48
Nightlight	49
The Dining Couple	50
Italian Delicatessen	51
Snakes & Ladders	52
Visitation	53
Touched	54
Night Walk	55
Snakepit	56
Two Admirations	57
Old Testament	58
Just Before Waking	59
Necrophiliac	60
Faith	61
Grave Light	62
The Gulf	63
By the Seine	64
Not Working	65
Kismet	66
xx	67
Underwritten	68
Succubus	69
Consanguinity	70
Isthmus	71
Connected	72
The Fossil Record	73
Settling	74
About the Author	77

Winter

The cold has driven in the mice
to scratch like over eager spies
behind the bedroom skirting board.

Unobserved, unsurveyed, but I sense
their awareness in the dark;
a ring closed by claws tiny and dry
as the points of leaves driven by the wind's
changing, all-pervasive frequency.

The iron voice of a winter, boundless,
calling along all the long- and short-lived spines.

Twilight

Time falls with grace
when the birds' fine
threadscrews of song
work out the light.

Flaking stucco the day,
revealing the ancient
arabesques of night
those little birds have traced.

Cadence

To hear that brook
decades gone in the twilight
 again;
to see the furrows
of that field bright
under the Moon...

To hear and see them
without the burden I was,
to have them erase
the burden I am...

To have the purity, the arrest,
the hidden cadence,
these glimmering tokens of memory
 hint of.

Nocturne

Soon gone
and nothing
I can do
about it.
Like the brush
of a beautiful body
in the street,
but slower,
not a finger
I can lay upon it.

The load of night
ineffable in its glide,
majestic, unruffleable,
keeping mum
to the ends
of its dark
softly shining hair.

The Passing Sky

What can the passing sky tell me?
Or the frond-tips of the pine
like undersea flora wavering at the light?

What has the bird to say?
Hopping like a refugee through the leaf-burned
 branches.
What's in the wind's sullen scourings?

There is no sustenance. Sing cold February
 away.

Cornwall Winter

Flickering lambency
from one afternoon back then.
Friendship there untorn,
torn love whole.
And the Sun stopped
the spheres ground
to a halt.
Just the clouded
stilled atmospheric
winter country
boundless around
our pub table
of huddled, firelit glass.

Winter

All Summer's orchards are grey rubble
in Winter's vast frozen contours.
But stubbornly I stare at the fire
whose flames leap though they're encased.

And I see the bright skins of Summer fruit
in the crevasses of the crumbling logs.
Though all is Winter and Winter is a circle
without circumference, whose centre is everywhere.

Searching

The Moon leans
out of space,
peeps over the cloud
like a mother
into a cradle.
Then turns away
with steelier light,
with a look infinitely
elsewhere.

Flowing Away

A strange bed
in a strange room
in a rustling sarcophagus
 of leaves
unconcerned, letting
the withdrawing tide
of the hours flow.
Watching the sky's
surreptitious surge
into the sea
pass without note.
The susurrant dark
drown the unrecorded light.
The world turn
into space.

Odalisque

Dream-soaked elegance
in sheets of night-cloud
the odalisque copper Moon
trails her jewelled light
lazily in the sea water.

A peasant mortal I'm filled
with fever at this display
of the local cosmic aristocracy's
self-sufficiency, élan.

She pulls her luscious amber light
out of the mud of my perception
and leaves me, bereft,
on the sand scorned and stained.

The Wild Sea

The sea heaving up
all along the seafront,
seaweed marinated
party-streamers
fired across the grass
made wetland.

Further down it rears
insanely,
tearing its white shirt
sharply against
the piled rocks.
Salt flying everywhere
like a fine rain of blood
when bombs go off.

And how fine
this violence,
pure as a leopard's
at the kill.
A vast innocence
that would snap the neck,
sweep that small boy away.

Unfolding

To fold out
along the creases and fault-lines
like a spring blossom.

To drift
with the delicacy of a snowflake
with mermaid feet
above the shards
of the broken world.

To persist
a nucleus of self
beautifully complete in itself

the way it was somehow meant.

Hedgehog

Spikes and snout
and ears tuned
to the wavelength
of earthworms.

Eyes wound
to the Moon's bright thread
that I follow
into my own
pallisaded dark.

And cut
this eternal winter
out.

Spring Rain

Dateless, the rain,
softening, washing
Now to timelessness.

Years, life, all
is music I've yet to read,
while I lie, listening

to the darkness drumming.

Candleflame

Two inches of candleflame left
of the day;
this yellow knife-tip so firm,
soon, in seconds, to be smoke.

Its brightness, almost of the Sun,
in the silence, is a tabernacle,
a Holy of Holies, containing
in a wafer, all the years.

Blackbird

The light has left
the blackbird's beak,
its song is tucked
beneath its wing.

Would that Sun and I
were as closely tied.
To sleep with it, and wake;
without this worm

between my teeth.

Wood-Pigeon

I kneel, poised with a match,
to light the logs leaning
in the soot-framed fireplace.
A wood-pigeon's notes
funnelled from somewhere close
rise to startle me.
That common, ungainly bird,
so comic, overweight on its trapeze of branches.
But these few notes, so cool,
so intimate, yet so disembodied...
They seem the very voice
of all the summers lived,
and the life in all the years
I never knew.

Clipped

A ball of a bird
its heart everywhere
in the cage of my body
thumps.

Without song, without flight,
but hurtling along;
its trajectory the sky's
grave.

Gods

For all our youthful insight
neither of us could've guessed
that from the vantage-point of middle-age
we were gods on Olympus

solving life, solving ourselves,
on all those idle, wasted afternoons;
with skies as white and featureless
and as questioning as this.

Moth

I'm the moth who
wants to get out
away from the light

into and as far as
the dark stretches.

For all the light is
is my wings' dance

broken on a nail.

Unconscientious Objector

The dying Sun bombards
the dull building
making it blaze with golden light.

Above, the half-Moon soars
high, cold, like an aimless shell.

Below, in the fields
of the endless undeclared war
I wish by a raped tree

that here was elsewhere
and everything other.

Duality

The sand falls
and no hands
can stop it
or contain it.
The sifting sound
is me; the sand
my body.

Emptiness

Not completely empty.
Life is too subtle for that.
There's a dreg of wine
in the bottle
and another broken half
snoring in the other room
whose serrated edge

will never fit to mine.
And in my mind
the litter of the long party
fresh as the emblaze
of lipstick on a glass.

No More Black Magic

Slumped, glum,
but I can feel
Time pass.

The day's grey pallor
turns yellow
like a corpse
getting healthy.

And our talk
makes light
of how miserable I am.

Even depression
will not stick
no matter how much life
I try to breathe into it.

Time will run the blackest
of black dogs
thin.

The Fog Horn

The fog horn
warns the ships
but the rocks
and currents
are all here
in thousands
of lit living rooms
inshore of the coast,
where the slowest
of living deaths is.

Honeycomb

To comb honey
out of memory
in a beehive hut...

Alone beyond the hum,
working the gold out
of all the horror...

Busy, sealing the wall
between the world
and my hermitage
of one.

Backbone of the Nation

Like some fat
little octopus
bleeding ink
the small businessman
squats at the bar
talking big.
But worse than him
is the small
willing audience
suckered
to his fat little tentacles,
in awe
of his pullulating sac
of noxious acumen.

I want to wade in,
stab and cut,
strike a blow
for everything formless,
undeliverable, equivocal;
but sit back, drink,
endure his trumpeting.
Not out of weakness, or strength,
but resignation;
the small businessman
is of another species.

Conversation

My tongue rattles
like a painter's brush
but none of its colour
reaches him, across the table.
He smiles, sparkles with assent even,
but his mind is elsewhere.
Roving his own gallery of finished pictures,
selecting one he can present to me.
My turn to smile, and look away,
fixing him with appreciative noise.

Sunset

A panorama of air brushed
by the slow loss of the Sun.
Its hurt, a delicate glory,
that finds its legs in me, for a moment.

Orienteering

If passing time were only
not like a rock-slide
in which you struggle for footing,
and the whole mountain
  not moving.
And if there were only
not that one stone with your name on it,
indistinguishable from the rest
that will put paid to all your efforts...

You will never stand straight.
And here's the Moon,
its features broken and smeared
by time's unrelenting violence
to remind; but shining
with its own slipping radiance.

Salute to Li Po

I sit
with beer
in the spirit
of Li Po's wine

and no better company.
His words
on the page

deep as footprints
in the snow
up Heaven's Gate mountain.

Loophole

A soul window, a worm-hole
out of mechanic time
before another morning...
Let me skip between the gears
out to where the airy waters
are unchurned, are still...
Let me be a gnat, a leaf,
drooping over its own reflection there,
or better still, the Moon's
silvered face, whole, unbroken,
on a dark plane where the mill
of the world means nothing.

Underworld

Sea of myriad dark suns
descend, rest upon my tired eyes
like a low cloud upon the hills.

And let my fingers feel
the cracked seal of a shapeless door,
and when I push let it swing

into the shade of a great orchard
whose ever-ripening, never-staling fruit
thickens the darkness.

And let some Proserpine bring me
draught after draught
of that Elysian cider.

Arboreal Meditation

Nerves torn out
and grafted to a tree trunk.
Bulges of feeling
wrapped in bark
and left to bake
in the winter Sun.

Let the birds, insects, termites,
 have it,
the banked, useless desires,
let them break it like bread
in the sunlight and fly,
and prove me useful.

Florescence

I should go mad
over one flower;
put it in a glass
and watch it open,
water it with rapture.

I should let one flower
ignite in me a passion
that can never fade.
I should let them
lock me away,
arms wrapped at my back.

I should, with my one bloom,
become uncontainable

Aphrodite Dictates

Worship, not love, til the idol
or the ardour crumbles.
Worship, not love, give
your passionate madness, take
no other currency. Worship
not love, love requires compromise
while worship's indivisible, divine, causes
divinity in the self, gilds
the idol with gold. Worship,
not love, to partake of the gods,
we, who are beyond reason.

The Unbleached Blonde

She has gold snakes
on her head, all natural;
but they don't seem
to do her any good.

Maybe they're too tight;
maybe they're too heavy;
maybe she'd prefer silver
to gold,
or another form of reptile.

That coiled mass of gold
glints at me like something
underground, forbidden…
If only I could unweave one lock,
feel what is so intimately
connected
is so intimately independent of her.

Rosary

Like fingers
smoothing a rosary
her legs
beneath the table.

Beauty is holiness
in those crossed bones
that has nothing
to do with her

that I burn for.

Nightlight

The flame of the night-light
beats in its thick red glass;
image of our twinned tongues,
closeted, unwinding to their common root.

Oh to be in you, wick in flame,
curtained from all the world,
all our old refractions fused,
as wave by wave we move, deeper into love.

The Dining Couple

He wishes the table was a continent
she wishes it was the handle of an oyster knife.
He stuffs the food in like it was mouthfuls of chain
and munching could shorten his sentence.

She loads butter on the hands and feet
of a poppet of bread
and talks him through his drowning
with a mouthful of red wine.

Visitation

She was an angel to me
as I sat, erect
on the four-poster bed,
her wings beating her up
and down on my shaft;
her spread, strained feathers
drawing me to heaven
as the fire cracked and spat.

Touched

Her brush is a claw
that fires my blood;
from that one point
she walks all over me.

And I, over her, coil
supinely; lost to the inside
and outside of myself.

Night Walk

The whole vast night Sea
leaving your small stretch
of footprint, repeatedly.

As we tread the soft new sand
created by the interlocking tides
of imagination and memory.

Snakepit

As real as the fire
your pale limbs
coiled round me
in a cove
of the impossible.

Your sap sings
so sweetly attuned to me
as we lie hotly
entwined in a pause.

Listening to the crashing
foam of the world
grow ever more remote...
Until there's only our breath

laughing, licking round
everything
that's left.

Two Admirations

I

Such limbs
of perfectly joined
blonde wood
moving without strings.

Lying here
limp with desire
I am the puppet.

II

In me the children
blossom and fall
like fireworks
as she leans toward me
unintentional
across the table

on the other side
of the Universe.

Old Testament

I am the bush
burning for you
though you never
asked for a miracle.

I am a pillar of fire
by night
against which
you could rest your head
if you wanted to.

By day
I am Lot's wife
turned to salt
for always looking back.

At dusk
I am Eve
packing in the fallen garden
pining for the snake
that had your face.

Just Before Waking

She was pushing me
in some kind of bath chair
in the dream.

She let down her warm hand
in a lace glove
beside my face.

I gripped it sadly,
kissed it,
she pulled it away,

and pushed me on
along the strand
to where the Sun broke

on this the bright expanse
of our eternal separation.

Necrophiliac

Let me make you
dead to me,
let this night
be your tomb...

But before the lid
let me plant a kiss...

Now Love, rot
within this seal
of forgetfulness...

Quick now! Quick!
Crowbar and torch!

Faith

He clings
to that bit
of her face
like a cripple
to the relic
of a saint.

He rubs
his hope upon it
and dare not look away.
For the rest of life,
ugly,
is creeping up
her body.

Grave Light

Down to the dark
of the grave
without the light
of the eyes of the girl
across the bar.

Down to the grave
I must repair
unprepared
while the light of their eyes
criss-crosses above.

But in the lightless soil I'm safe
and the worm is eternal love
sightless,
and no sting in her tail.

The Gulf

Her swift removal
of the dying flowers
says it all.
The emptied vase
to me is death
not the decaying petals.
Those insanitary heads
on drooping stems
spread shadowy luxuriant life
by candlelight.
A little thing
that touches me
more than her.

By the Seine

Her hair was champagne yellow,
loose as our love,
of ageless vintage.

In that shaded, tiled, ratty cafe
down from Notre Dame
that probably isn't there anymore,
where we let time go to Hell.

Where we sat with sunlight trapped
in our champagne glasses
as traffic passed along the Quays.

And the words rose,
indistinguishable from thought,
easy up my sloping sides,
to rest in the haven of her lips, her eyes.

Not Working

Odd that we couldn't make it work
all those years ago.
But not odd in that
I didn't believe in work then,
and don't believe in it now.

It isn't work that turned you,
so antithetical to me,
into this ageless presence, waiting
at the edge of a remembered
rain-washed field,
that I can love now.

Kismet

The surreptitious caress
she gives my face –
is it the brush of her love
from the courts
of a previous life?

Did we scratch and bite
and kiss through the night
of a Sun not this? No. This
is the previous life,
our magnetism's just the dawning

the sunrise of a timeless
many-fingered love
which was always destined.

XX

Two Xs in the white space
of the computer screen
put me in mind of bird imprints
in the freshly washed sand
we both flew over, light as air,
long ago.

These tiny grey crosses,
useless as bent nails,
to me are vast scars
in the heart's landscape
to exult over
that no sea can ever erase.

Underwritten

She underwrites
my existence
though the ink
on the last signature's
 fading.

And I'll never
get another.
I must fill
the crude squiggle
with my love's
invisible ink.

And keep on holding
my heart
in the fire.

Succubus

I feel your hips,
your arse, your thighs,
in the dark, all
without moving.

I feel the eyes
of your breasts brush
my closed lids,
your mouth give me breath,

though your lips are closed
on the other side of the Sea.

Consanguinity

Out of the blue
you nudge me
like a faraway twin.
The perfect complement,
so perfect
you're folded
out of reach.
But thinking of you
my beating heart
draws you in;
until we're pressed close,
exactly opposite
against the night's dark screen.
I feel your blood knock,
and all of me,
thrilling,
answers you.

Isthmus

My heart flooded
into the channel
that opened accidentally
as we sat pressed
back to back at the bar.

An isthmus, it seemed,
between my continent
of loneliness and hers.
There was no traffic.
But when I looked at the spot

at the bar tonight
my sealed spine burned.

Connected

The wind rushing, cold and deep,
her face frail as a leaf,
its branch my stubbornness.

A river parts further each second
we who were never together
and by no stretch can be.

But this thread of connectivity glows
like a worm in the dark,
the tearing wind its bellows.

The Fossil Record

Beneath her feet of clay
miles away
my heart turns
into a fossil.

All I am is hers
but it will never
make her heart
skip a beat.

I can only listen
to the dying echo
of her retreat
as the wet clay

hardens into horn.

Settling

I'll settle for you
faceless, bodiless,
a whiff of
immanent perfume.

I'll settle for you
as thin rib of memory
with wings of
gossamer possibility.

I'll settle for you
as hook, as hinge,
on which desire swings
never finding rest.

About the Author

Born in Liverpool in 1959, JOHN McKEOWN is an English/History graduate of John Moore's University and an alumnus of the city's seminal Dead Good Poets Society. He lived in Prague in the 1990s where he was part of the city's expat literary scene. In 2000 he moved to Dublin, becoming a columnist for *The Irish Examiner*, and arts feature writer for *In Dublin* and *The Irish Times*. He was theatre critic for the *Irish Daily Mail* from 2006 to 2008, and since then has reviewed theatre for *The Irish Independent*.

His poems have appeared in *Orbis, The Frogmore Papers, Dreamcatcher, Other Poetry, Earth Love, Envoi, Borderlines, The London Magazine, Cyphers, The Shop*, and *Southword*. His work also appears in *The Return of Kral Majales (The King of the May): Prague's Literary Renaissance 1990-2010*. This is his fourth collection, after *Looking Toward Inis Oirr* (South Tipperary Arts 2004), *Amour Improper* (Hub Editions 2004), and *Sea of Leaves* (Waterloo Press 2009).